Dedication

This story is dedicated to pet parents everywhere who make sure their pet's needs are met.

Every dog needs a safe and cozy place to rest. Cats do, too!

A big thank you also to those special folks who provide shelter for feral cats so they can be comfortable as well!

Hardcover ISBN: 978-1-965929-16-2
Paperback ISBN: 978-1-965929-17-9
Coloring Book ISBN: 978-1-965929-18-6

www.casatransport.org

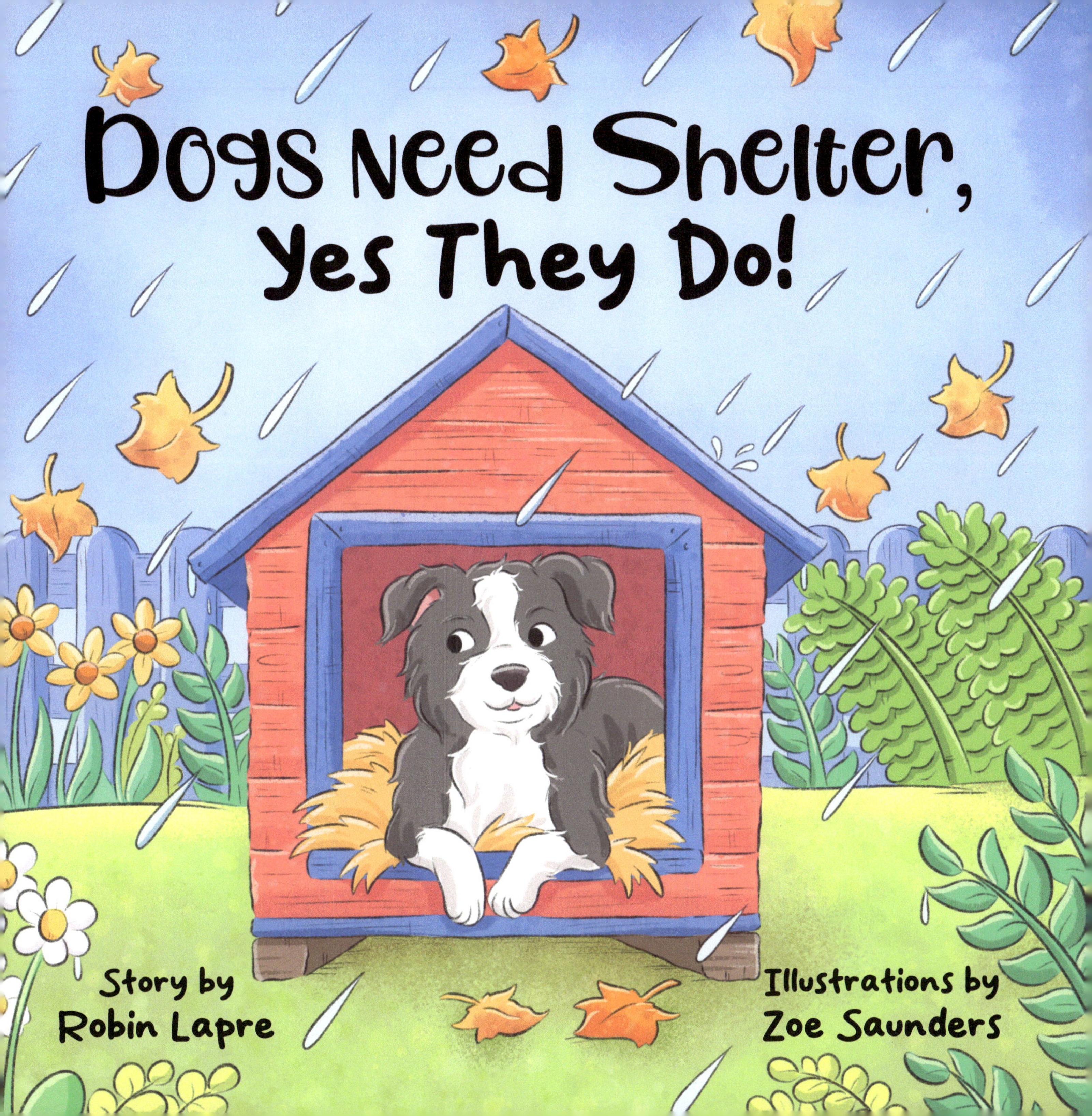

Dogs Need Shelter, Yes They Do!
Story by Robin Lapre
Illustrations by Zoe Saunders

Every critter needs a place
That meets their needs and gives them space.
Dogs might live high, dogs might live low,
But all dogs need a place to go.

Dogs might be indoors, might be out,
That's what this story is about.
No matter where they live, it's true,
All dogs need shelter, yes, they do!

In the summer, dogs need shelter
From the heat so they won't swelter.
Make sure there's a shady spot
Where they can go if they get hot.

BAILEY

And put a pail of water out
So they can dip their thirsty snout.
But if the sun is way too strong,
Then bring them in where they belong!

If tired, panting, warm to touch,
Your dog is saying, "It's too much!"
The roads get hot and burn their feet.
Beware of danger from the heat.

The winter chill is also tough,
And sometimes fur is not enough!
Dogs need a tarp to block the wind.
But if it's frigid, bring them in!

It's true that some dogs love a freeze,
The Huskies and Great Pyrenees!
But short-haired dogs get much too cold,
The young, the small, the very old.

And if your dog is always out,
They'll need a place to rest, no doubt.
A doghouse should be stuffed with straw.
All dogs need shelter — that's the law!

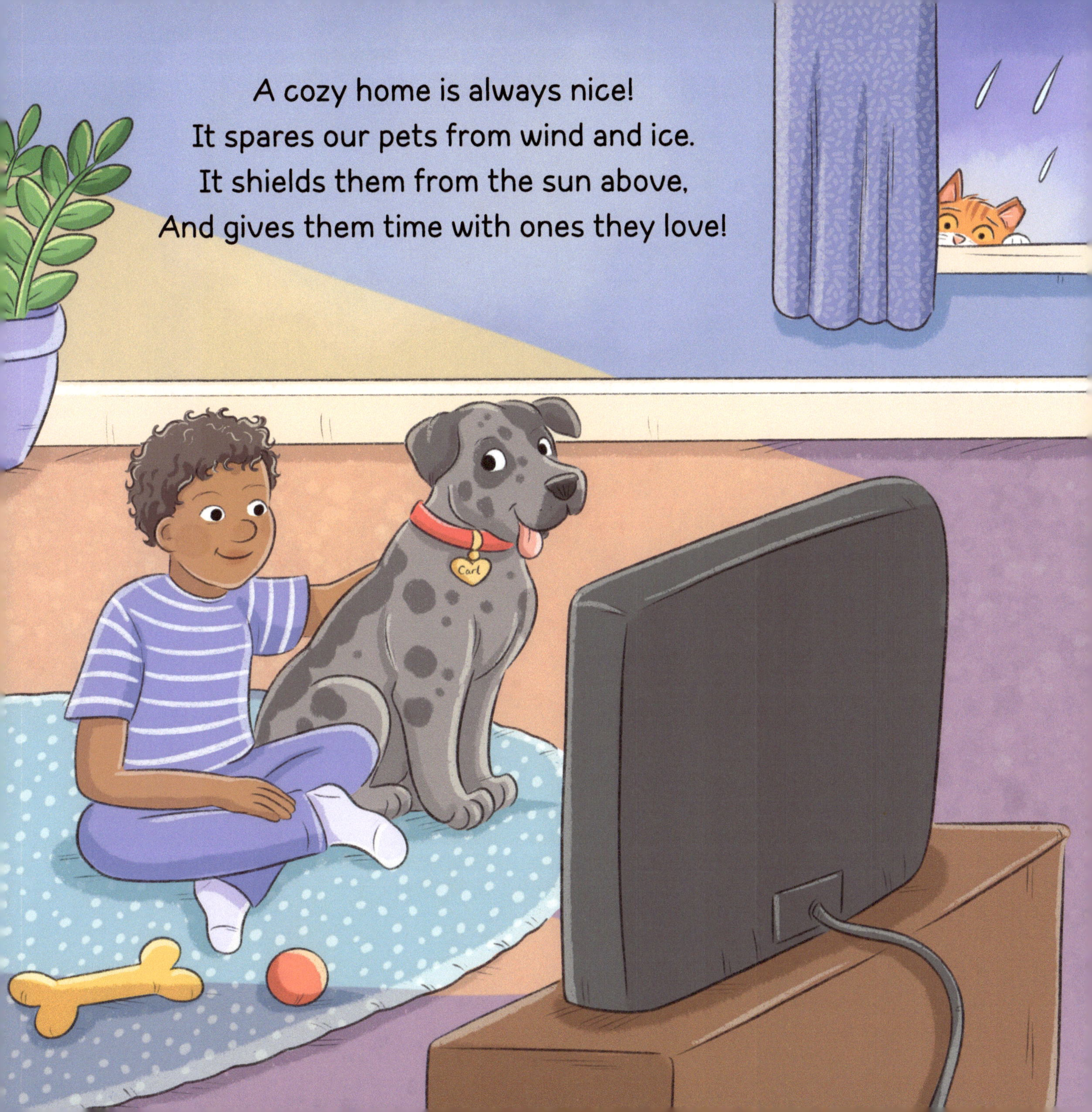

A cozy home is always nice!
It spares our pets from wind and ice.
It shields them from the sun above,
And gives them time with ones they love!

Do indoor hazards lurk? You bet!
So watch for things that pose a threat.
Like medicine and cleaners too,
And pick up stuff your dogs can chew.

FRESH 'N' CLEAN
SOFT 'N' SNUG
GERM AWAY

And don't forget the feral cat!
She lives outside. She's cool with that.
She doesn't want to play with you,
But here is something you can do.
*A feral cat is an outdoor cat
that stays away from people.

In winter, when the temps run low,
She'll need a place where she can go.
A box, a hole, a place to rest.
Just add some straw, you've made a nest!

"Now, about those heavy chains," dogs say,
"We don't like being tied all day!"
It's even worse when weather's bad.
Just bring them in, and they'll be glad.

Yes, every critter needs a home,
A place to call their very own.
Where they feel safe, and they can rest,
And weather doesn't get them stressed.

So stand up tall and say it clear,
And shout it loud for all to hear.
"For every dog and cat alive,
They all need shelter to survive!"

Discussion Questions

1. Why is shelter important for animals?

2. How can you tell if your dog is getting too hot?

3. Which dogs have an extra hard time in the cold?

4. How can you make a doghouse comfortable for a dog?

5. Why shouldn't we leave dogs on a chain all day?

6. How can we keep dogs safe inside?

7. Why do outdoor cats need shelter?

*This cat's flat ear tip means she has been fixed.

Discussion Answers

1. Shelter is important because it keeps animals safe and comfortable. A good shelter keeps animals dry and not too hot or cold. It also keeps them safe from other animals.

2. Your dog may be too hot if they are panting and tired. They may look for shade and water. Dogs can get very sick if they overheat, and their paws can get burned from hot pavement.

3. Dogs with short hair get cold easily, as do small dogs. Watch out for shivering! Dogs that are very old or very young also should not be left in the cold. Even huskies and dogs that like the snow need to be watched. Make sure their water hasn't turned to ice!

4. A doghouse should be made of good materials with an opening away from the wind. Straw bedding is very important for warmth. We don't use hay or blankets in a doghouse because they can get wet and make dogs cold. Raising a doghouse a few inches off the ground keeps it warmer inside.

5. Dogs don't like being on a chain all day because they can't run and play freely. Chains can be very heavy and get tangled. This makes dogs sad and scared. If you must tie up your dog for part of the day, a cable tether is more comfortable for dogs.

6. When dogs are inside, we need to keep them safe. This means putting away cleaners, medicine, or even chocolate and grapes which can make dogs sick. Pick up small toys so they don't choke on them. Make sure your plants are safe for pets.

7. Outdoor cats need shelter because they can get cold and wet. They need a safe place to hide from wild animals and even other cats. You can make a cat shelter with a box or chest lined with Styrofoam and filled with straw. Make a 6-inch hole so they can get in and out!

About the Author

Robin Lapre is a wife, mom, physician, and animal lover.

After years of volunteering at animal shelters, Robin saw the need to educate children about the basic care of cats and dogs. Specifically, she teaches responsible pet ownership, a topic that is rarely taught, and we feel the consequences in overcrowded shelters everywhere.

Look for these titles with more to come, as CASA continues to Promote Animal Welfare Stories!

Doggie Do's and Don'ts as Told by Cadence the Dog

Two Frisky Kittens: How to Count High Real Quick

I Like Kibble and So Much More!

I Lost My Cat! Now What?

What Do All Dogs Need to Drink?

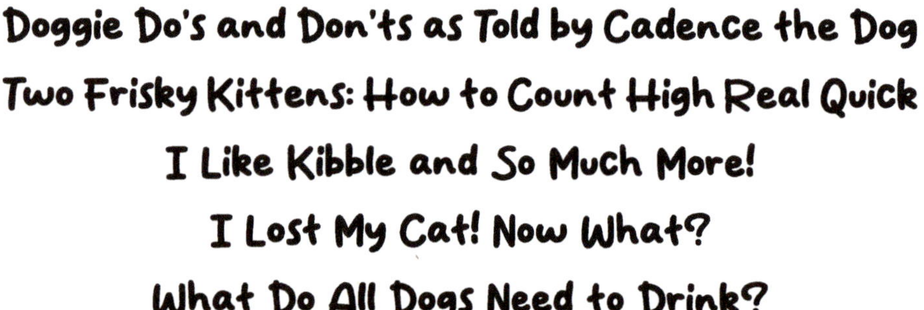

Casa Transport

These books are made possible through the support of Charlie's Angels Saving Animals (CASA), a nonprofit organization in Tennessee that helps many animals each year through rescue transport and low-cost spay/neuter services. CASA has taught thousands of students about responsible pet ownership under the initiative known as CASA PAWS (Promoting Animal Welfare Stories).

Visit **www.casatransport.org** to read more about this amazing organization, and follow us on Facebook at **CASA PAWS** and Instagram **@paws4casa**.

www.ingramcontent.com/pod-product-compliance
Lightning Source LLC
Chambersburg PA
CBHW042127030726
47599CB00002B/382